MACHINES MADE SIMPLE

Wheels

Written by E.C. Andrews

KidHaven
PUBLISHING

Published in 2026 by
KidHaven Publishing, an Imprint of
Greenhaven Publishing, LLC
2544 Clinton St., Buffalo, NY 14224

Written by: E.C. Andrews
Edited by: Elise Carraway
Designed by: Amelia Harris

Cataloging-in-Publication Data
Names: Andrews, E. C. (Children's author)
Title: Wheels / E.C. Andrews.
Description: Buffalo, NY : KidHaven Publishing, 2026. | Series: Machines made simple | Includes glossary and index.
Identifiers: ISBN 9781534550841 (pbk.) | ISBN 9781534550858 (library bound) | ISBN 9781534550865 (ebook)
Subjects: LCSH: Wheels--Juvenile literature. | Axles--Juvenile literature. | Simple machines--Juvenile literature.
Classification: LCC TL412.A62 2026 | DDC 621.8--dc23

Manufactured in the United States of America

CPSIA compliance information: Batch #CSKH26
For further information contact Greenhaven Publishing LLC at 1-844-317-7404.

Please visit our website, www.greenhavenpublishing.com.
For a free color catalog of all our high-quality books, call toll free 1-844-317-7404 or fax 1-844-317-7405.

Find us on

Image Credits
All images are courtesy of Shutterstock.com, unless otherwise stated. Cover – Manolo1312, GLYPHstock, trekandshoot, eamesBot. Recurring images – Onica Alexandru Sergiu. 2–3 – Heavypong. 4–5 – Fahroni, popcatter, Jeanette Virginia Goh, Juice Flair, ODE.Studio. 6–7 – Red_Shadow, Rapax, Gereti Studio, Drozd Irina, Louella938. 8–9 – Scharfsinn, zhengzaishuru, John O'Neill, (User:Jjron), CC0, via Wikimedia Commons. 10–11 – Cara Kate. 12–13 – Ireshetnikov54, LuckyYouPhoto. 14–15 – Sergei Kazakov, wavebreakmedia, IAMSUTHICHA. 16–17 – TheVanya43, Ryzhkov Oleksandr, evakerrigan, LN team. 18–19 – Ruslan Kerimov, Rudmer Zwerver, Bekker24. 20–21 – Nattapol Meechart, Om.Nom.Nom. 22–23 – Erickson Stock, Dejan Dundjerski, adriaticfoto.

Contents

WORDS THAT LOOK LIKE THIS CAN BE FOUND IN THE GLOSSARY ON PAGE 24.

Marvelous Machinery

What comes to mind when you think about machines? Is it computers? Maybe it is cars? Perhaps you think of super cool crime-fighting robots! These are all machines. However, a lot of machines are much simpler.

Machines have been around for a very long time. We use different kinds of machines every day. You probably use machines at school, at home, and while you are playing without even realizing it.

What Is a Machine?

A machine is something that is made to help people do certain tasks. Machines can be used to make lifting things easier. They can be used to move things from place to place.

WINCHES ARE USED FOR PULLING HEAVY THINGS ALONG.

Simple machines are the most basic kind of machines. They affect the strength or direction of a force. Wheels, levers, and wedges are all simple machines.

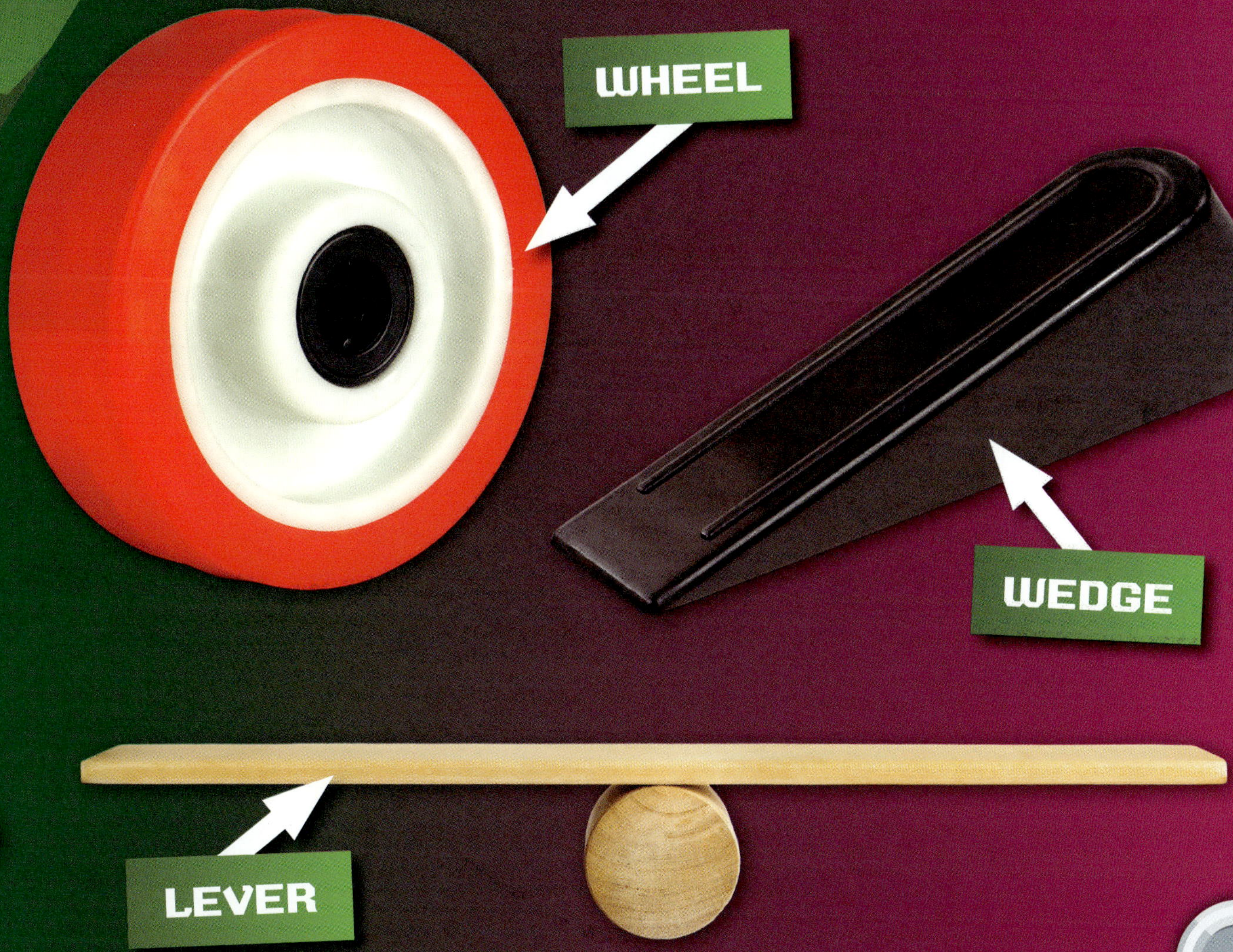

What Is a Wheel?

A wheel is a round object. It allows things to roll or spin around. The wheel is one of the oldest machines in the world. It is also one of the most important.

Without wheels, many other machines would stop working. Cars, trains, and tractors would not be able to move or do their jobs. Wheels are used inside smaller machines, such as clocks.

CLOCKS HAVE JAGGED WHEELS INSIDE THEM CALLED COGS OR GEARS.

Parts of a Wheel

Most wheels have a part in the middle that rotates or that they rotate around. Some wheels have other parts too.

Rim

A rim is the outside of a wheel. The rim has a circular shape that allows the wheel to roll.

Spokes

Some wheels have spokes. Spokes are long pieces of material that connect the middle of the wheel to the rim around the outside. They also stop the wheel from <u>collapsing</u>.

Axles

Wheels often spin around an axle going through the center. An axle is a cylinder-shaped rod. Axles hold wheels in place. They allow wheels to be attached to larger machines.

Bearings

Some wheels have bearings. Bearings are small metal balls that roll against the axle or wheel as it spins. Bearings allow a wheel to turn smoothly around an axle.

BALL BEARINGS WORK LIKE TINY WHEELS.

BALL BEARINGS

Working with Wheels

Friction is a force that happens when two objects scrape against each other. Friction slows the movement of objects. Lots of friction can stop movement altogether. Wheels lower the amount of friction.

Wheels cause less friction by rolling over the ground instead of dragging across it. The rolling movement means that less material touches the ground. This stops the material from digging in and dragging.

Wheely Useful

Transport Wheels

Every day, we use wheels for moving things around—including ourselves! Machines such as bicycles, cars, and trains have lots of complicated parts. However, they would not be able to move at all without wheels.

RUBBER TIRES ON THE WHEELS OF CARS AND BICYCLES GIVE BETTER GRIP AND A LESS BUMPY RIDE.

Farming and Building

People use machines such as tractors and combines on farms. Machines such as diggers and cranes are used to build things. All these machines need wheels to move around and work.

THIS PART OF A CRANE IS CALLED A PULLEY WHEEL.

COMBINE

DIGGER

Wonderfully Fun Wheels

Ferris Wheels

Wheels can be used to make fun things too. Ferris wheels are big wheel-and-axle machines. They are held together with strong spokes. There is a thick axle in the middle that allows the wheel to turn.

Rollercoasters

Rollercoasters have wheels that run along tracks. Many rollercoasters have two sets of wheels on the top and bottom of the track. This allows rollercoasters to turn upside down. This is called inversion.

Wheels at Home

Musical Wheels

Record players are machines that play music using a wheel called a platter. The platter spins the record around. A needle drags across the grooves of the record as the platter spins. This creates the sound.

Computer Wheels

Platters are still used inside some game consoles and computers. Wheels also turn the fans in these devices. These fans look like spoked wheels. As the fans spin, they push air around the machine.

THIS STOPS THE MACHINE FROM GETTING TOO HOT.

Super Simple

Simple machines can be used as part of much bigger and more complicated machines. From wheelbarrows to roller skates, we use simple machines every day. Not all simple machines we use are visible at first.

CAN YOU SPOT THE SIMPLE MACHINE ON THIS WHEELBARROW?

There are a lot of simple machines in your home and classroom. You probably use them every day without realizing it. Have you used any wheels today?

Glossary

collapsing	falling in on itself
cylinder	a 3D shape with a top and bottom in the shape of a circle
force	a push or pull on an object
rod	a thin, straight bar, especially made from wood or metal
rotates	spins around

Index